The Futura Library of Comic Speeches

SPORT

1. Comic Speeches for Sportsmen

D0465646

Also from Futura

The Futura Library of Comic Speeches
2. COMIC SPEECHES FOR SOCIAL OCCASIONS

The Futura Library of Comic Speeches

SPORT

1. Comic Speeches for Sportsmen

Futura

A Futura Book

Copyright © Victorama 1986

First published in Great Britain in 1986
by Futura Publications, a Division of
Macdonald & Co (Publishers) Ltd
London & Sydney
Reprinted 1987

ISBN 0 7088 2985 6

Typeset by Leaper & Gard Ltd., Bristol
Printed and bound in Great Britain by
Collins, Glasgow

Futura Publications
A Division of
Macdonald & Co (Publishers) Ltd
Greater London House
Hampstead Road
London NW1 7QX

A BPCC plc Company

Contents

PART ONE

*How to make a
comic speech*

Ground Rules

Be heard. Be understood. Be enjoyed! Believe it or not, those three simple rules hold the key to making a successful public speech. Observe them and you have nothing to fear. It couldn't be much easier, could it?

Unfortunately, as hundreds of public speakers have found to their cost, standing up in front of an audience of strangers and trying to make them laugh can be a nerve-shattering experience. There are those speakers who mumble and falter and forget their words, leaving the audience without the faintest idea of what they are talking about. There are those who tell unsuitable jokes and stories which, at best, embarrass those listening and, at worst, provoke uproar. And there are those who don't bother to prepare their material and just drone on for as long as the fancy takes them about anything that comes into their heads — and then they wonder why their audience has fallen asleep!

The chapters that follow will show you how to avoid these common pitfalls. But much more than that, you'll find in them all you'll need to make a successful comic speech — everything from how to assess your audience and the material that will entertain them, to how to prepare and organize your speech and deliver it with confidence. And, of course, there are pages of stories, anecdotes and quotations to ensure that you're never at a loss for a joke.

Know your Audience

No matter how nervous you feel about it, remember that it's an honour to be invited to speak in front of an audience — so acknowledge the fact by creating a speech specially designed for the occasion. A rambling, irrelevant performance that has nothing to do with the occasion or those listening to you verges on the insulting. What your audience will want to hear, and you should aim to provide, are effortless, amusing stories and ideas — stories and ideas that are of direct interest and relevance to them.

Some speakers like to think that they have perfected a kind of general-purpose speech; a speech which, with a few minor alterations and additions, will go down with any audience and on any occasion. It may be useful to have a few ready phrases and jokes to hand if you suspect that you're going to be asked to make an impromptu speech, but this kind of general-purpose material won't set an audience alight. They'll sense its general nature and the fact that no great imagination or thought has gone into it — and if the speaker is unlucky some of them will have heard him perform it elsewhere!

What this means is that for every occasion and every audience you need to create a new speech. But before you sit down and start to write it, spare a few seconds' thought to work out just what's required.

The Audience

You may be keen on cricket and your cricketing jokes may have gone down brilliantly at the sports club dinner — but they are unlikely to have the same appeal for the guests at a wedding or the ladies of the Townswomen's Guild. Obvious? It doesn't seem to occur to a great number of speakers that it's the audience who will determine whether their material is funny or not. And if the audience don't like your jokes you might as well give up. So make sure that you choose the right material by finding out about the people you'll be speaking to.

Age is an important factor. If you know that your audience will be young and sophisticated, choose some of the more sophisticated material in this book and, if necessary, update some of the details. Likewise, if your audience is past retiring age adapt the jokes and stories to suit them. Try not to tell jokes about Boy George to audiences who remember Victor Sylvester!

An all-male gathering is likely to enjoy rather more robust material than an all-female gathering — but that doesn't mean that you can feel free to tell dirty jokes simply because the audience is all-male. Never offend those who are listening to you. If you suspect that your material might prove offense to anyone at all, then cut it. And if *you're* embarrassed by any of your material, leave it out. Your embarrassment will communicate itself to the audience and then *they'll* feel embarrassed for you.

The members of the local bird-watching club will want to hear a speech that reflects their interests. This doesn't necessarily mean that every word you utter must be about birds, but don't be tempted to throw in a completely irrelevant joke just because it's funny. Most jokes can be adapted to fit almost any topic, but if you can't slide a story neatly into your speech you'd do better to leave it out. You don't want your audience to be worrying about your joke about cannibals — and what it has to do with them — as you try to continue with the rest of the speech!

If you have been asked to speak at a formal function where you don't know the audience, find out as much as you can about the people expected to attend — particularly, if it's appropriate, the names and titles of those on the organizing committee. Do a little homework and see if you can come up with any interesting or amusing stories about them or other guests, and weave these into the fabric of your speech. This will prove that you've worked hard to create a special speech for the occasion and your audience will respond to the personal touches.

The Occasion

Different occasions require different kinds of speeches, and you'll find details about what kind of speech is most appropriate for the major social occasions in the last part of this section of the book. But it isn't just the formal requirements of an occasion that matter when it comes to preparing your speech.

The tone of the occasion is all-important too. A vote of thanks at a rugby club when the team has just topped the local league will be quite different in tone to a vote of thanks at an afternoon business meeting. Try to assess what the mood of your audience will be. Will they be ready for a belly-laugh and a funny story about the chairman, or will a more wry and sophisticated kind of humour best suit the occasion? Make up your mind which to go for and choose your material accordingly.

It's also worthwhile bearing in mind the fact that if you've been asked to speak it's probably for a purpose. Whatever that purpose — whether it's to present a prize or propose a toast — you should never get so carried away with your own words that you forget to do it. Learn from the story of the speaker who, having stood up to give a five-minute presentation speech, sat down again still holding the award half an hour later! The best way of avoiding this kind of embarrassment is to plan your speech carefully and then stick to it. Try to resist the temptation, no matter how well you're being received, to improvise. It's improvisation that is likely to throw you off your stride.

Here's a simple check list of 10 Do's and Don't's which you should bear in mind as you sit down to prepare your speech.

Do's

1 Do check the age and sex ratio of the audience.
2 Do find out what your particular function is to be. Have you been asked to propose a toast or make an after-dinner speech? Make sure that you prepare the right kind of speech.
3 Do find out how long you will be expected to speak.
4 Do some homework on any special guests or members of the audience.
5 Do adapt your material to suit the occasion.

Don't's

1 Don't use old material.
2 Don't risk offending anyone with blue jokes.
3 Don't speak for too long and don't try to improvise.
4 Don't include irrelevant material.
5 Don't forget to fulfil your function. If you've been asked to make a toast or offer a vote of thanks then remember to do so.

Perfect Preparation

Once you know the kind of speech you're going to make and the sort of audience you'll be entertaining, you can begin to prepare your material. Preparation is absolutely vital if you're going to give a polished performance, so allow as much time as possible to work on the speech.

Start by reading through this book and jotting down all the jokes, quotes, anecdotes and so on that you like and that you feel are directly relevant to your audience. Be ruthless and cut out anything that isn't related in some way to your subject and anything that can't be adapted to fit. On a separate sheet, put down all the things that you *have* to say in the speech and all the points that you particularly want to make.

With any luck you'll begin to see the material falling into place, with the quotes leading into the points you want to make and the stories illustrating the theme. This is exactly what you're aiming for — a seamless speech with one idea moving into the next without any effort. You'll probably have to adapt some of the material if it's to fit in perfectly, so change the names and locations and details to suit the occasion. For example, if you're going to be speaking in Newcastle and you're using a joke set in London, change the location and add some Geordie colour. Most importantly of all, put everything into your own words. You'll feel more comfortable when you come to use the material if it's written in the kind of language and the style you're used to, and it will make your speech seem that much more personal to the audience.

Sir Thomas Beecham once said of his orchestra that the important thing was 'to begin and end together, what happens in between doesn't matter very much.' Pretty much the same can be said of making a speech. If you can capture the attention of the audience with your first line, you're likely to have them with you for the rest of the speech. And if they're going to remember anything when they get home it's likely to be your final line — so make sure that it's worth remembering.

Some speakers like to work on the opening and closing lines of their speech together, linking them so that the last line finishes what the first line started. Whatever you decide to do, make sure that both the beginning and the end of your speech are absolutely relevant — both to the occasion and the central part of the speech. Nothing irrelevant should be allowed in at all or you'll begin to look as if you're rambling.

Opening and closing a speech are the two most difficult things of all. If a brilliant opening occurs to you then use it — but if nothing original springs to mind, try using one of these opening gambits.

Quotations

You'll find dozens of useful quotations in this book and one of them should be ideal for opening your speech. When you're looking for it, bear in mind that it should allow you to move straight into the main part of your speech without any stress. If you have to force a quotation to fit your theme then forget it. Always inform your audience that it *is* a quote and not your own words. It's quite likely that someone in the audience will have heard it before and they might think you a fraud if you don't name the person who said it first.

Questions

A question can be a very effective way of getting your

speech off the ground. Try asking an apparently serious one and following it up with a ridiculous answer. Or ask a ridiculous question to which there's no answer. Whichever kind you choose, aim to raise a laugh from the audience and break the ice.

The 'Did you know?' gambit is also a useful one. Find an amazing fact in the relevant section of this book and ask your audience if they knew it. It's bound to start your speech off with a bang!

Jokes

A joke may seem the obvious way of starting a speech, but in fact jokes can go badly wrong. If they work you'll have the audience eating out of your hand — but if they fall flat you'll have everyone in an agony of embarrassment and praying that you finish quickly.

The best kind of joke to look out for is one that has something to do with a member of the audience or with something directly relevant to the occasion. You may find that simply by changing a few details in one of the jokes in this book you've got the ideal opening gag — in which case use it. But never use a joke simply because *you* think it's funny.

Ending a speech with a joke is even more risky than opening with one. After all, even if your opening joke falls flat you have the rest of your speech to regain the audience's interest. If you end with a damp squib, however, no matter how good the speech the audience will remember you for only one thing — your failure to pull it off. Only finish with a joke if you can think of nothing better and if you're absolutely certain that it will work.

Exactly the same advice can be applied to ending a speech. No speech, no matter how well-received can be counted a great success unless it ends on a high note. Looking for a new screenplay, Sam Goldwyn once remarked, 'What we want is a story that begins with an earthquake and builds up to a climax.' That's what you have to aim for too!

Never end with an apologetic, 'Well, folks, that's about it,' line. That only suggests that you've run out of ideas or that you couldn't be bothered to finish the job off properly, and there's really no excuse for that. Even if you can't find the kind of climax that Goldwyn was looking for, you *can* end you speech in an amusing and tidy way.

Quotations

Don't use a quotation for the opening *and* closing of your speech because that would look too much like cheating, but a quote can round off a speech perfectly. Again, you'll find something suitable in the relevant section of this book — and again, make sure that it ties in completely with the main subject of your speech.

Anecdotes

There's bound to be an anecdote in this book that will encapsulate and illustrate your theme perfectly. You can use it to finish your speech in classic style, but beware of using anything too long or rambling. You don't want to lose your audience's attention in the last few moments. If you're speaking about friends, family or colleagues at work, try to uncover an amusing story about them; nothing embarrassing, of course, just something to show what nice people they are. This is *guaranteed* to bring your speech to a successful conclusion.

When you're preparing your speech, take an occasional look at this checklist of 10 Do's and Don't's just to keep your aims in mind.

Do's

1 Do check your material to ensure that it's suitable for the audience you assessed in the last section.
2 Do make sure that you have included all the things you *have* to say — your vote of thanks or the toast, for example.
3 Do adapt all the material to ensure that it's relevant.
4 Do aim to start and finish your speech on a high note.
5 Do credit any quotations you use.

Don't's

1 Don't use any material that isn't relevant to the occasion or will cause offence.
2 Don't start your speech with a joke unless you feel confident that it will work.
3 Don't tail off at the end of the speech; finish properly.
4 Don't use too many quotes or anecdotes from the lives of other people.
5 Don't speak too long; make sure that your speech is the right length.

If, when you finish preparing your speech, you feel confident that you've observed these guidelines, you can be sure that you're halfway towards success. Now all you need to know is how to deliver the speech you've written!

Successful Delivery

Preparing your speech is one thing — and the most important of all — but delivering it is something else. The best
speech can be ruined by poor delivery and the thoroughly
mediocre made to pass muster by good technique. Fortunately just a few simple measures will ensure that your
delivery does your speech justice.

Rehearsal

You don't need to learn your material like an actor, but
rehearsal will help you to become familiar with it and iron
out any problems that weren't apparent on paper. For
example, you may find that a particular sequence of words
turn out to be difficult to say, or you might have problems
pronouncing certain words — in which case find alternat-
ives. Try to learn half a dozen key phrases which will take
you smoothly from one part of your speech to the next so
that you don't keep having to refer to your notes; no matter
how nervous you're feeling, this will make your speech
seem smooth and practised.

While you're rehearsing, experiment by using your voice
to emphasise different points of the speech. Try changing
your tone and volume, too, for effect. If you have a tape
recorder then use it to tape the various versions of your
speech — then you can play them back and decide which
sounds the most interesting and lively. Don't, by the way,

worry about your accent. Lots of speakers try to iron out their natural accent, but they forget that the way they speak is all part of their personality. Without it they seem very dull. As you listen to yourself speaking you'll begin to recognise the most successful ways of delivering certain parts of your speech. For example, the best way of telling your jokes is to do it casually, without labouring them too much. If you feel that there's a rather dull patch in the speech try animating it by changing your tone or emphasis, or even just speeding it up a bit. It's this kind of preparation that will give you polish on the day.

Body language

No matter how nervous you feel about speaking in front of an audience, you should try not to let them know — and it's the body which most often gives the secret away.

Begin by standing easily with your weight on both feet so that you feel balanced. This way you'll look steady, even if you don't feel it. Your main problem will be what to do with your hands. If you have notes, hold them in front of you at about waist level with one hand. With your free hand, lightly grasp the note-holding wrist. If you're lucky, there will be a lectern of some sort at which you can stand. Rest your hands on either side of it and you'll look very much at ease. Only royalty can get away with holding their hands behind their backs, and you'll look sloppy if you put your hands in your pockets, so don't adopt either of these postures. If you've no notes and no lectern, just stand with your left hand lightly holding your right wrist in front of you. It looks surprisingly natural and relaxed. Next time you switch on the TV you'll notice how many presenters and comedians use the position!

Notes

The very worst thing you can do is *read* your speech. Comic speeches need a touch of spontaneity, even if they've been prepared weeks in advance and you've been rehearsing for days. Reading a speech kills it dead. It makes the material seem dull, even if it isn't; it prevents eye contact, which is very important in breaking down the barrier between speaker and audience; and it destroys that important sense of a shared occasion, with speaker and audience responding to each other. On top of all that, the very fact that you are reading will indicate a lack of confidence — and your audience will be alerted to your discomfort and share in it.

That said, it's equally inadvisable to stand up and speak without the aid of any notes at all. Nerves can affect the memories of even professional speakers, so don't take any risks. Many people like to write their notes on postcards, using a single main heading and a couple of key phrases to prompt them. If you decide to do this, make sure that you number the cards clearly. You are bound to drop them if you don't, and reassembling them in the wrong order could create all kinds of chaos! Make sure, too, that you write your headings in large capital letters. When you're standing up and holding the cards at waist level you need to take in all the information at a single glance.

If cards seem too fiddly, write the main headings of your speech on a single sheet of paper, again using a few key words underneath to jog your memory. You'll know, from your rehearsals, those things you find difficult to remember and those which come easily. Jot down the point you get stuck on.

If you're going to use quotations then write them clearly on postcards and read them when the time comes. This ensures that you get them absolutely right and, far from doubting your competence, your audience will be impressed by your thoroughness.

Don't try to hide your notes. Simply use them as inconspicuously as possible. They prove that you have prepared a speech specially for the occasion and that you care about getting it right — and there's no need to be concerned about that.

On the day

On the day of your speech there are a number of simple precautions you can take to ensure that everything goes smoothly. Some of them may seem quite painfully obvious, but it's the most obvious things that are overlooked, particularly when you're nervous.

The most basic precaution of all is to ensure that you arrive at the right place at the right time. If you can get there a little early you'll be able to check out the acoustics and the arrangements. For example, will you be speaking from a podium or simply standing up at the table? Is there a microphone — and if so, do you know how to work it? If you've had time to think these things through you're less likely to be flustered by them.

Wear the right kind of clothes. You'll feel very uncomfortable if you turn up to a black-tie dinner in your second-best suit, so make sure that you're correctly dressed for the occasion and that everything about you is neat and tidy. You don't have to look like a fashion plate; you simply have to avoid anything distracting. It's a good idea to slip off to the cloakroom before your time comes and check your appearance. There's nothing like a tuft of hair sticking up from the top of your head to take the audience's mind off what you're saying.

While you're in the cloakroom, use the chance to go to the loo. Nerves affect different people in different ways, but it's better to be safe than sorry!

If you know that you tend to put your hands in your pockets while you're speaking, remove all your loose change and keys so that you're not tempted to jangle them. And make sure that you have a clean handkerchief somewhere about you. A scrap of well-used tissue isn't going to impress the audience when you need to blow your nose.

If you've worked hard to make the opening words of your speech interesting and funny, it would be a great shame to waste them by starting to speak while the audience is still talking and settling down in their seats. So wait for silence, even if it seems to take an age, and when you've obtained it start confidently and loudly so that everyone can hear what you have to say. Whatever you do, don't be hurried. Public speakers talk quite slowly and allow plenty of pauses so that the audience can respond. Take it at a leisurely pace, making sure that you're heard throughout the room, and you'll win the audience's attention immediately.

Some people, but only a *very* few, are at their best after a few drinks. Unless you know for certain that alcohol will improve your performance, it's probably best not to drink before you speak. Drinking tends to dull reactions and instil a false sense of confidence — and you need to be completely in control of yourself and your material if you're going to make a success of the occasion. Naturally, once you've made your speech and it's been greeted with success and laughter, you can reward yourself!

Whether you've been drinking or not, accidents do happen. Cope with them by acknowledging them and turning them to your advantage. For example, the speaker who knocked a glass of water over himself brought the house down with the throwaway line, 'Whoops! For a moment there I thought my trousers were on fire!' If someone in the audience drops a glass or falls off their chair, acknowledge it and pause for laughter rather than ploughing on as if nothing has happened. Although you have prepared your speech in advance, you should be aware of things happening around you and flexible enough to add a topical observation or funny remark if necessary. And the better-rehearsed and more at ease you are with your material, the

more confident you'll be about including the odd spontane-
ous line.

If you follow these guidelines you really can't go far
wrong. But here, as a last minute reminder, is a checklist of
Do's and Don't's that will ensure that your delivery will do
justice to all the work you've put into your speech.

Do's

1 Do rehearse your material.
2 Do work on your posture so that you look relaxed and
   comfortable.
3 Do prepare your notes and quotations carefully.
4 Do take simple precautions — like dressing correctly
   and checking your appearance.
5 Do anticipate any accidents and interruptions and be
   prepared for them.

Don't's

1 Don't read your speech.
2 Don't make any last-minute attempts to change your
   accent or your appearance.
3 Don't arrive late or unprepared.
4 Don't start your speech before everyone is ready.
5 Don't drink before you make your speech.

The Right Speech for the Right Occasion

The kind of speeches that sportsmen and women are most likely to have to make fall into two categories — after-dinner speeches and presentation speeches. Of course, you can use the jokes in this book for all kinds of purposes and not just for sporting events — but the most common sporting occasions when speeches are required are dinners and presentations.

After-dinner speeches

The after-dinner speaker doesn't have to propose toasts or give votes of thanks. He or she has only one job to perform, and that's to entertain the audience with an amusing speech for fiften minutes or so after dinner. After-dinner speeches are difficult because the speaker is entirely alone when he stands up and he has to be entertaining for some time. But they can also be very rewarding, giving you a chance to show your skill in front of a willing audience.

Preparation is the most important ingredient of an after-dinner speech, because if you can't speak confidently and amusingly for the prescribed time you're stuck. The moment a speaker gets boring or begins to ramble, he has failed in his task — which is to entertain. So for the after-dinner speaker above all others, the section on preparation which you'll find earlier in this book is vital reading.

The second most important ingredient is wit. Although after-dinner speakers can include a serious moment in their material, no one will want to hear anything too downbeat. Keep it funny — and you'll find no shortage of suitable jokes and anecdotes in this book.

The final ingredient is brevity. However well your speech seems to be going, don't be tempted to extend it. A short but wickedly amusing speech that keeps the audience spellbound is far better than a longer but only occasionally funny performance. If you should find that your speech doesn't seem to be going down as well as you'd hoped, and if after ten minutes or so things haven't picked up, then cut it short, conclude properly, and sit down. If an audience is determined not to enjoy you then there's no point in ploughing doggedly on. However, if you've done your preparation properly and practised your delivery, you should have no reason to fear a cool reception.

Presentations

Sportsmen and women seem to spend much of their time participating in competitions of one sort or another, so if you're in line to win an award or to present a trophy you'll be pleased to hear that presentation speeches are very simple indeed.

The most important thing about this kind of occasion is to give the audience the basic information it needs to understand what's going on — and very little more than that. If you're presenting the award, try not to go on for too long about it. The spotlight should fall on the sportsman or woman, not on you. By all means, if you know the recipient and you have a personal story to tell about him, then do so — just don't take too long.

There's a simple formula to follow for making a presentation:

1. Name the trophy or award and some details about it:
   The Puddleton and District Challenge Cup was first awarded in 1966 as a memorial to that great Puddleton and England darts player, Norman Pippin.
2. State the reason for the presentation:
   Each year the Cup is awarded to the team that tops the Puddleton and District Darts League.
3. State what the recipient has done to deserve the award:
   This year's winning team, who were an astounding eleven points clear at the top of the league, are from the Ferret and Firkin in Lower Puddleton. Eric Flight, their captain, is here this evening to receive the trophy on their behalf.
4. Present the award:
   It gives me great pleasure, Eric, to present you with this magnificent cup. Congratulations to you and to all the team.

If you're to be the recipient at this kind of presentation your reply should follow this pattern:

1. Say thank you:
   Thank you, Mr Smith and all the organisers of the Puddleton and District Darts League, for this lovely cup.
2. Acknowledge the donors or origins of the prize:
   Every darts player in Puddleton knows all about that great player Norman Pippin, and I and my team are very honoured to have won this trophy.
3. Say what you intend to do with the award:
   We will hang this cup up in pride of place above the bar at the Ferret and Firkin, and every time we look at it we will remember Norman Pippin.

Don't try to be modest if you've won an award and don't say that you can't think what you've done to merit it. People will either agree with you or think you're telling lies.

Should you be asked to speak at any other kind of function, the general guidelines offered in this section will still apply.

Find out from the organisers how long you'll be required to speak for and if there is any specific task that they want you to fulfil. Then, using this book, assess the kind of speech the audience and the occasion will require, prepare it using the jokes and anecdotes in the next section, and practise it until you feel confident. And good luck!

Here's a final checklist of Do's and Don't's to be considered when you're working out what kind of speech is required for a particular occasion.

Do's

1 Do consider the audience and the occasion.
2 Find out how long you're expected to speak for and, if necessary, on what subject.
3 Find out what kind of speech you are required to make.
4 Research all the necessary information including names, titles and clubs.
5 Be prepared, be witty, be brief.

Don't's

1 Don't, if you're making a presentation, hog the lime-light.
2 Don't forget to thank and acknowledge everyone who needs to be thanked and acknowledged.
3 Don't be over-effusive or falsely modest.
4 Don't forget to make clear notes of important names, facts and details.
5 Don't extend your prepared speech unless it's absolutely necessary.

PART TWO

The Material

In this part of the book you'll find all the material you need to create a comic speech for any kind of sporting occasion. There are jokes, quotes, facts and stories about almost every sport you can name, from football and cricket through to some more unusual recreations like croquet and curling, to ensure that you're never at a loss for a witty word.

Just Joking

Somewhere in this section you'll find the ideal jokes for your speech. When you find them, don't just lift them straight from the page. Adapt them so that they are completely relevant to the theme of your speech and add your own personal touch to the details. Last of all, rewrite them in your own words. By the time you've finished, you won't simply have borrowed them from this book — you'll have made them your own.

The coach of a local football team decided to take drastic measures to improve his players' performance. He lined up 11 dustbins on the pitch and told the players to dribble and pass the ball around them as if they were opponents. The dustbins won 3-2 after extra time.

Two men were trying to get into a crowded football stadium minutes before kick-off at a vital cup tie. One of them turned to the other and asked, 'Do you think we'll make it in?'
    'I certainly hope so,' said the other. 'I'm the bloody ref!'

In the dying minutes of the jungle soccer match the grasshopper bounded down the left wing looking for the winning goal. Quick as a flash a defending rhinoceros lunged out at the insect and pulverised him into the ground. The crowd went berserk and the referee, a wise old owl, called the offending rhino over. 'Right,' said the owl sternly, 'you've killed a player — you're off!'

'But ref,' protested the rhino, sobbing, 'it was an accident. I only meant to trip him!'

What do you call a brain surgeon who specialises in treating footballers?
A chiropodist.

The Irish football manger was explaining tactics to his side before the big cup final. 'Sure,' he said, 'we just have to make sure that we equalise before the other team scores.'

Did you hear about the soccer player who was stopped by the police for drinking and driving? The police officer went up to him and asked him to blow up a balloon. 'Certainly,' said the driver, 'who's playing goalie?'

An Irish goalkeeper was explaining why he never stopped a shot. He said he thought that was why the net was there.

The Irish football team had a poor season. The only success they had was when the pools panel chose them for a win.

A Liverpool fan was asked how he thought his team would fare in an upcoming cup tie.
'I think it will be three each,' he said confidently.
'Really,' said the reporter, 'three each?'
'Indeed,' said the fan. 'Three for Kenny Dalglish, three for Ian Rush, three for ...'

The goalie was having another poor day and had just let in his fifth goal of the match. One fan in particular was disgusted by the performance.
'How much does that joker get paid for doing his job?' he shouted. A fellow fan thought it was about £100 a week.
'Good God,' cried the first man, 'I know a carpenter who'd board the whole goal up for a tenner!'

The opposition crowd were giving the hard-pressed goalie in front of them a lot of useful advice.

'Move out to it,' 'Punch it clear,' 'Stay on your line,' they kept yelling. In the dying moments of the game a dashing forward bore down on the goal and threatened to score. The crowd was partly hushed in the tension of the moment when one of them called out loud and clear, 'Use your own discretion!'

Animals can be great sports fans. A man went to the pub with his dog just as the soccer results came up on TV. When the commentator announced that the local side had lost heavily, the dog started an almighty howling and could not be comforted.

'What's got into the animal?' asked a fellow drinker.

'He supports Rovers,' explained the dog's owner, 'and he always gets upset when they lose.'

'What happens when they win?'

'I've no idea,' said the man. 'I've only had him for 18 months.'

After 25 years of loyal support, a soccer fan gave up going to watch his local team. He claimed it was a complete waste of toilet paper.

Did you hear about the patriotic Brazilian woman who named her first-born son after the entire national football team? Apparently she wasn't sure which was the father . . .

And did you hear about the soccer team that bought a highly-rated Jewish striker? They had to sell him because he wouldn't give anyone the ball.

A football fan was bragging about his team's abilities to his rather dim girlfriend. 'We've got a great team — no losses, no draws and not a single goal conceded.'

'That's fantastic,' said his girlfriend. 'How many

matches have they played?'

'None yet,' said the fan. 'The season starts next week.'

The local prison has a great football team but there's just one small problem — they don't play away games.

An occasional supporter of a struggling lower division soccer team rang up the ground on match day. 'When's the kick-off?' he asked.

'When can you make it?' came the reply.

Deep in the tropical jungle the army patrol was in a tight spot. Pursued by enemy troops they had to cross a crocodile-infested river. The first three volunteers who tried to swim across were eaten by the crocs. In desperation the sergeant turned to one of his men. 'Private Wilkins, swim across with this rope.'

At this the captain, who was standing nearby, protested that this was not cricket, as the Private had not volunteered for the duty. 'It's all right, sir,' said the sergeant. 'Private Wilkins is a Bristol soccer fan.'

And before the captain could reply, they saw the soldier swim safely across with the rope. The crocodiles glanced at him only briefly as he splashed under their noses. 'What do you mean, he's a Bristol soccer fan?' asked the baffled captain.

'Look at his bum, sir,' said the sergeant. Both men looked across the river and saw, neatly tattooed on Wilkin's buttocks, *Bristol Rovers for the Cup* and *Bristol City for the League.*

'I see what you mean,' said the captain. 'Not even a crocodile could swallow that!'

A life-long Merseyside soccer fan joined the committee of Everton Supporters Club. His friend was disgusted.

'What the hell have you done that for?' he demanded. 'You've always been a Liverpool fan like me!'

'I know, I know, but I've just been to the doctor and he says that I've only got three months to live.'

'What's that got to do with it?' his friend asked.

'Well, I thought that if someone had to lose a member I'd rather it was those bastards at Everton!'

A striker who had a good reputation as a scorer both on and off the field, finally decided to hang up his boots and look for new employment. Although he was keen to get a job he was also rather fussy about what he took on — and the Job Centre had a lot of trouble finding work for him. Eventually they called him up and asked him if he'd mind working abroad.

The player umm-ed and aah-ed and finally said he'd give it a go. Did they have any more details? The official said they didn't; all they knew was that it was well-paid work, with expenses, somewhere in the Middle East.

So the soccer player flew out and arrived at a luxurious palace in the middle of the desert, where he was greeted by the chief adviser to the local Arab prince.

'You are here,' said the adviser, 'to impregnate 80 maidens of my master's choice. For each of them you will be paid £20 plus expenses.'

'That's bloody typical of the Job Centre, isn't it?' the striker said bitterly. 'They send you all this way for two days' work!'

Two old pals, Bill and George, had been going to watch Spurs play for donkey's years. One season however, Bill failed to turn up at their usual spot on the terraces. This happened four times in a row, so George went round to see Bill and find out what was the matter.

'I'm very sorry, George,' said Bill, 'but over the summer I married a very randy woman. Just as I'm about to leave for the match she grabs hold of me and . . .'

George was furious. 'Don't let yourself be bossed around like this,' he instructed. 'Next time she tries that move, pick her up, take off her knickers and spank her hard. Then go to the game.' Bill agreed to try this.

The next week there was another home match and, once again, Bill failed to turn up for it. George stormed round to his friend's house. 'Why didn't you do what I said?' he demanded.

'But I did!' Bill protested. 'When she grabbed me I put her over my knee, took down her knickers and ... Well, Spurs haven't been playing too well lately, have they?'

An elderly sportsman, in his day a great athlete and performer, loyally supported his local football side through thick and thin. Alas, their record became so bad that they were regarded by many as little more than a joke side.

As the old chap lay on his death bed he called the club president to him. 'Look here,' he gasped, 'I've been a loyal fan and always come up with the cash when you've needed it, haven't I?'

'Oh yes!' said the president. 'You've always been a faithful patron to us.'

'In that case,' the dying man said quietly, 'would you do a favour for me?'

'Of course, what is it?'

'I'd be very grateful if the players would all gather on my grave when I'm gone, as a sign of remembrance.'

'That's a fine idea!' cried the club president. 'Where are you to be buried?'

'At sea,' the old man murmured. 'At sea ...'

Overheard on a golf course ...
GOLFER: My wife says golf is my religion.
FRIEND: Why's that?
GOLFER: I always play on Sundays.

A young priest was on the golf course — and having great difficulty in hitting the ball. Try as he might he couldn't make contact. In desperation he began to pray for help, but still he missed the ball. Once more he launched into a prayer as he lined up the shot yet again — but still the ball didn't move. His wily old caddie sidled up to him.

'Look, father,' he whispered, 'when you pray, keep your head down!'

To broaden his game a young American golfer came to Britain to try out some famous British courses. His first was St Andrews and he arrived on the first tee expecting a great game. He positioned himself, took a great swipe — and missed the ball. He tried again, took a nuge swing, and missed once more. 'Gee,' he said, turing to his embarrassed companion, 'is this a tough course!'

Another poor golfer was hacking his way around a course, digging out divots as he went. About half-way round, as he removed another massive piece of turf as he tried to hit the ball, he turned suddenly to his caddie. 'You know,' he said, 'I'd move heaven and earth to break 100 this round.'

'Then you'd better try heaven,' muttered the caddie. 'That's all that's left.'

Members of a golf club were horrified to see one of their players carrying the dead body of his companion on his shoulders as he came back from the links. The club president spoke for all of them when he said, 'It must have been a terrible experience, having to bring him back dead like that.'

'Oh, it wasn't that so much,' said the surviving golfer. 'It was having to pick him up and put him down again between holes.'

Bored with heaven, Moses and Jesus came down to earth for a round of golf. On the third hole part of the fairway was covered by a lake and Jesus decided to make an approach shot over it with an eight-iron.

'You're nuts' said Moses. 'It will never reach.'

'What do you mean?' asked Jesus. 'Arnold Palmer uses

an eight-iron, doesn't he?' And with that he chipped the ball — which fell straight into the lake. 'Okay, Moses,' said Jesus, 'just part the waters so that I can go and fetch the ball, will you?'

'Forget it,' said Moses. 'I told you it wouldn't reach. Go and do your walking on the water bit and fetch it yourself.'

Jesus refused and tried the shot again. 'If Arnold Plamer can do it, so can I.' But once more the ball plonked straight into the water. He tried again, but still couldn't make the far shore. Finally, worried about the number of balls he was losing, he agreed to fetch them himself and walked out onto the water to collect them. Just then a bemused couple who have been playing a few holes behind them came up and stood near Moses. 'Who the hell does that guy think he is?' asked the man, 'Jesus Christ?'

'No,' exclaimed Moses turning round. 'Ruddy Arnold Palmer.'

Two men who have been golfing buddies for years were finally parted by death. One night the ghost of the dead golfer appeared to his friend. 'Good news,' said the ghost. 'They've got a fantastic course up here. The bad news is you're booked in there first thing tomorrow!'

The colonel and the vicar were playing golf together for the first time. Trying to drive off at the first tee the colonel missed the ball. 'Sod it, missed!' he exclaimed. The vicar took a very dim view of this language and told the colonel so. But some minutes later the colonel failed with an important putt and again exclaimed, 'Sod it!'

This time the vicar was really furious. 'I'm telling you, Colonel, God is not mocked. If you can't control your language something terrible will happen.'

His companion took the point and, deciding that discretion is the greater part of valour, managed to control himself. Then, on the final green, he found himself faced with an easy six-inch putt to win the game. He approached it carefully — and fluffed it. Then he began swearing like a demon.

Suddenly there was a tremendous thunderclap and the vicar was hit by a bolt of lightning, which killed him where he stood. In the distance the colonel heard a deep rumbling sound ... 'Sod it, missed!'

Did you hear about the Irish golfer who managed to lodge his ball in an oak tree? He used a tree iron to get it down.

After they had unsuccessfully searched the rough for nearly an hour and still not found their balls, the two young golfers were about to give up when an old lady, who had been watching them, came nervously over.

'Forgive me for intruding,' she said, 'but would it be against the rules if I were to tell you where the balls are?'

Two friends were enjoying a round of golf. One of them took from his bag a new invention which he had just come across — an unloseable golf ball.

'If you hit it into the trees or the rough and can't find it, you just yell and it will give out a little bleeping noise,' he explained.

'Is that all?' said the other man.

'Not at all. It can float on water and for evening games it glows in the dark.'

'That's terrific,' exclaimed the other man, impressed. 'Where did you buy it?'

'Buy it?' asked the first man. 'I didn't *buy* it, I found it!'

Two sports entrepreneurs were travelling in Africa when they were shown a remarkable sight by the local witch doctor — a gorilla which could play golf. The African explained that he had taught the creature how to hit the ball from birth, and with its natural strength it could propel the ball for miles. The two Americans, sensing a great publicity coup, paid the witch doctor a huge sum to allow them to take the gorilla back to the USA. After a few strings were pulled, the gorilla was entered for the US Open — and as it arrived on the course it caused the desired stir. The animal lined up on the first tee, a par five hole, and hit a magnificent shot which travelled 450 yards down the fairway to lie right next to the hole.

The crowd were amazed and watched delightedly as the gorilla walked to the hole and, taking a putter from the caddie, prepared for its next shot. The animal took aim, swung the putter . . . and hit the ball another 450 yards to the next hole.

A golf news item: 'As in previous years, the evening concluded with a toast to the new president, in champagne provided by the retiring president, drunk as usual at midnight.'

Two Jewish golfers decided to go on a golfing tour of South America. Alas, things began to go disastrously wrong from their very first day on tour, and after serious problems at customs they found themselves in front of a firing squad at dawn.

As they were being tied to the posts the captain came up to the first golfer and asked if he had a last request. He said that he hadn't. The captain then went to the second golfer and asked if he had a last request. Instead of replying, the man spat in his face.

'Stop it, Arnie,' whispered his golfing companion. 'Do you want to get us in trouble or something?'

A young girl from a poor country family was taken to visit rich relatives, a wealthy middle-class couple. As she entered the house she saw two old golf balls lying in a box.

'What are those?' she asked.

'They're golf balls,' her uncle explained. The girl took note of this information, and about a year later when she visited once more she noticed that there were now four golf balls in the box.

'Oh look, everyone!' she exclaimed. 'Uncle's shot another golf!'

A young British golfer on the world circuit went to play in a small Arab state in a little-known tournament. One day, after finishing a round, he met a fellow countryman who was working there in an oil refinery.

'What do you do with all your spare time out here?' asked the golfer. 'You must go out of your mind with boredom.'

'Not at all,' replied his new friend. 'We have a great time. For instance, today if Tuesday when they bring in the booze. Want to come round for a piss-up tonight?' The golfer explained that he rarely drank.

'Hang on until Thursday, then' said the oil worker. 'That's the day they bring in the women.' The golfer went red and said that he wasn't interested. 'You're not gay, are you?' asked the man.

'Certainly not,' said the golfer indignantly. 'The very thought of it disgusts me.'

'In that case,' said the oil man, 'you'd better not hang around for Saturday night . . .'

Two anglers, who'd established a bet of £30 on who would catch the first fish, were sitting side by side on the river bank. Suddenly one of them saw his float twitch, but he got so excited that he managed to fall in the water.

'Christ!' shouted his companion in disgust. 'If you're going to dive in after the buggers the bet's off!'

An angler was lying seriously ill in hospital with injuries to his legs when the doctor came up. 'First the bad news,' said the doctor. 'You're going to lose both legs.'

The angler groaned. 'And what's the good news, Doctor?'

'A patient two beds along wants to buy your wellies.'

Two likely lads went fishing one day. As teatime approached one asked the other, 'What did you bring for supper then?'

'Let's see.' He looked in his bag and reported, 'Two bottles of whisky, a bottle of rum, a crate of beer and three lettuce sandwiches.'

'Good God,' said the other, 'what are you going to do with all that food?'

Two anglers were sitting on a bank waiting for a bite. One said, 'I pity that poor Noah. He was never able to fish.'

'Why not?' asked the other.

'With only two worms?'

The mourners were following the coffin of an angler's wife through the cemetery. On top of it lay a long rod and some tackle.

'That's odd,' said one mourner to his bereaved friend. 'I didn't know that your Elsie was interested in fishing.'

'She wasn't,' said the widower. 'I've got a match at three o'clock.'

A scruffy young boy was sitting on the kerb, apparently fishing from a rusty old bucket. A kindly old man came up and asked him what he was doing.

'I'm fishing,' said the child.

'How silly of me not to realise,' said the old chap, feeling sorry for the boy. He tossed a coin into the bucket. 'And how many have you caught today?'

'You're the fourth so far,' said the boy.

FIRST ANGLER: I hooked a mermaid the other day: What a figure!

SECOND: Really? What were the measurements?

FIRST ANGLER: 36-22 and 80 pence a pound.

A man met his old fishing pal walking down the street, his arm in a sling and using crutches.

'What happened?' he asked.

'It was my wife,' said his friend. 'She found out about that fishing trip I went on.'

'So?'

'She found out I didn't go on it.'

Two men were fishing at sea when one of them hooked a mermaid. He hauled her aboard, examined her beautiful body for a moment, then threw her back into the waves.

'Why?' asked his friend.

'How?' he replied.

'I've had terrible news,' said a man in the pub. 'My wife has just run off with my best mate.'

'That's awful,' sympathised the man next to him. 'What'll you do?'

'I suppose I'll have to go fishing without him.'

A fisherman's story . . . 'I caught the most marvellous pike,' said one fisherman to another. 'You should have seen it — ten inches.'

'Ten inches? That's nothing, I've caught plenty that size,' his friend replied.

'Between the ears?'

Despite hours of preparation the angler failed to get a single nibble all day, so on the way home he went into the pub to drown his sorrows. Sitting there and drinking more than was good for him, he became more and more angry with the world in general. As he stood to leave his eyes fell on a massive stuffed fish in a glass case above the bar.

'And whoever caught that fish,' he yelled drunkenly, 'is a bloody liar!'

An Englishman went to Ireland to do a spot of fishing. He came upon a suitable spot by a river and prepared to wade into the murky water with his wellies. But before he did so he asked a farmer who was mending a fence nearby if the water was shallow.

'Sure, that water's quite shallow,' came the reply. With this the angler walked straight into the river — and found himself up to his neck.

'You said it was shallow!' he cried as he waded out, completely soaked.

'To be sure,' said the farmer, 'and I thought it was. It only comes up to the waists of the ducks, and they're only six inches tall!'

Did you hear about the Irish Test match that had to be abandoned the other day? Both teams turned up in white.

A batsman's wife was very upset after listening to the cricket commentary on Radio Three. However, she was later reassured that the commentator had actually said that the wicketkeeper had whipped her husband's *bails* off . . .

A young boy rushed up to a spectator at a Yorkshire cricket match. 'Dad, Dad,' he yelled, 'I've got terrible news for you. Jimmy's got tetanus, grandma's dead and mother's run off with the postman!'

The man looked down at his son. 'Ay, lad, and I've got even worse news for thee — Hutton's out!'

The batsman sidled up to the bowler. 'Ere, mate,' he whispered, 'how about bowling a nice slow one I can hit? My wife's over there watching, see?'

'I'd be glad to help,' said the bowler, 'but I don't reckon you'll hit her from here.'

Just as the bowler was about to run up to bowl, the batsman put out his arm to stop him, stood bolt upright and took off his cap. Puzzled by this behaviour the bowler and fielders looked round and saw a hearse slowly drawing past the ground. They all joined in this tribute and after a minute everyone resumed training.

At the end of the over the bowler went up to the batsman. 'I must say,' he said, 'I thought that was a very touching and respectful gesture. Very touching indeed.'

'Well it was the least I could do,' said the batsman. 'After all, we were married for 25 years.'

Just before a vital cricket match a Cambridge college side discovered that they were one man short. They scrounged around and managed to find a brilliant local player who was, unfortunately, not very bright.

'Make sure that the opposition don't get to speak to you for too long and you'll be all right,' the skipper told him. 'No one will notice.'

Next day the game went ahead and, sure enough, the new recruit scored a splendid hundred for the college team — and won them the match. During drinks afterwards both teams got chatting and the opposition skipper came over to congratulate the young player on his fine innings. Then he asked what he was studying at university. The young man racked his brains for a moment, then inspiration struck. 'I'm studying sums,' he said.

The manager of a potentially rowdy cricket tour made a strict rule about keeping a diary on his team's behaviour. One day the captain of the team had a few drinks too many and the manager duly recorded, 'Captain drunk today.' When the captain complained he defended himself saying, 'It was the truth and I had to write it down.' A few days later the captain asked to make an entry in the diary. The manager, anxious to be fair, agreed — and was appalled to read, 'The manager was sober today.' Furious, he rushed to the captain and demanded an explanation. 'Well,' said the captain, 'it was true and I had to write it down.'

The tearaway fast bowler flew in to the wicket and hurled a delivery which hit the nervous young batsman plumb in front of the stumps. Everyone appealed loudly but to the bowler's amazement the umpire declared it not out. So the bowler tried again and delivered an even faster ball which once more only failed to bowl the batsman by hitting his pads. Again, the umpire turned down the appeal.

The bowler, furious by this time, took an even longer run, stormed in and bowled a ball that knocked all three stumps clean out of the ground. The bowler immediately turned around on the umpire. 'Nearly had him that time,' he snarled.

Ireland were playing England at Twickenham and the usual contingent of fans came over from the Emerald Isle for the weekend. One fan, staying at a London hotel, called the maid to his room to complain.

'It's my sleeping bag,' he said. 'I can't find the zip.'

'I'm not surprised,' said the maid sharply. 'It's a duvet.'

As expected, the crucial rugby match between the Archbishop's XV and the Pope's XV proved to be a finely-balanced contest. The Archbishop's side had all the tries, while the Pope's team had all the conversions.

A beery rugby player got home after a lengthy session in the pub with the team. 'Is my dinner warm?' he asked his wife as he burst into the bedroom where she was lying asleep.

'Only if the dustbin's on fire,' she growled.

An Irish rugby player visiting London for the weekend phoned the Salvation Army. 'Do you really save fallen women?' he asked.

'Yes, that's part of our work,' said a kindly voice on the other end of the phone.

'Great,' said the Irishman. 'Would you save a couple for me on Friday night?'

A vicar stood watching his first-ever rugby match. Pretty soon things got a bit nasty and at a line-out one forward turned round and punched the other right in the balls. The vicar turned to his companion on the touchline and said, puzzled, 'I wonder, can you tell me . . . How did one player know the other was a bar steward?'

A superstitious fly-half went to consult a fortune-teller about the prospects for the next day's crucial rugby match. 'Tell me, what do you see in the crystal ball?' he asked her.

'I see a large white van,' said the woman.

'What else?'

'I can also see a man standing there in a white coat.'

'This doesn't sound too good,' said the player. 'Is there anything else?'

'Yes, I see you lying on a stretcher.'

'That's it,' said the fly-half, 'I'm not playing tomorrow, it's far too dangerous.' And despite great attempts by the rest of the team to get him to play, he stayed at home all day. Inevitably they lost.

Later that evening he decided that it was safe enough to venture out and made his way to the pub. On his way he was run over by an ice-cream van.

Sign in an Irish rugby club: 'We open at 9.30 a.m. and close at 11 p.m. on the dot. If you still haven't had enough to drink in that period the proprietors feel you can't have been trying.'

An Irish weightlifter was given a dope test at the World Championships — and passed.

Did you hear about the unfortunate hurdler? He mistook the high hurdles for the low hurdles and shattered his personal best.

And have you heard about the unfortunate athlete who shot himself shortly after winning the Olympic marathon? It was a false start.

The organisation EXIT has arranged two new events for the next Olympics — catching the javelin and heading the shot.

Did you hear about the cyclist who collapsed and died after winning the Tour de France! It wasn't the race that killed him — it was the lap of honour.

Darts players are famous for their interest in food and drink. The girlfriend of one large player said one night, 'Say something soft and sweet to me, darling.'
'Black Forest Gateau,' he whispered.

A well-oiled darts player staggered home one evening to be met in the hall by his furious wife. 'I demand an explanation — and I want the truth,' she shouted.
'Well make up your mind,' said the darts player.

One darts player to another: 'Would it cause problems if you went home late and drunk again tonight?'
'Not really. I was planning to have my front teeth out, anyway.'

'No swimming on a full stomach,' the swimming coach warned his team after lunch. Five minutes later he returned to the pool — to find them all swimming on their backs.

A sportsman went to the doctor, saying he thought his diet wasn't healthy enough and was making him ill. 'What do you eat in the mornings?' asked the doctor.
'Snooker balls,' said the sportsman. 'Two reds, a yellow, and a brown.'
'Lunch?'
'Two pinks, a red and a blue.'
'Tea?'
'A black and three reds.'
'It's obvious what the matter is,' said the doctor.
'What is it?' asked the sportsman.
'You're not getting enough greens.'

A travelling salesman's car broke down and stranded him in a remote little town, so he booked himself into the only hotel for the night. It was a seedy old place; the TV was broken and there was no one in the bar, but as he passed one door he noticed an old snooker table and decided to have a solitary game.

When he asked about balls and cue the barman handed over a set of balls so old and dirty that they were a uniform grey in colour. 'How do you expect me to play with these?' the guest asked. 'I can't even tell the white from the black.'

'That's all right,' said the barman. 'You'll soon get to know them by their shape.'

Two Irish snooker players were on a national tour giving exhibition matches. One evening, with no game to play, they found themselves stuck in a small country town with nothing to do. Patrick suddenly got up and left the pub in which they were sitting, declaring that he was going to confession. Mick told him he was mad, but off Patrick strolled.

In the confessional, he told the priest that he'd made love to a local girl. Naturally concerned, the priest quizzed him as to who this girl was — but Patrick refused to say and eventually left.

'Well, Pat,' said his friend when he returned to the pub, 'did you get absolution?'

'Indeed I didn't,' said Patrick. 'But I got some useful names and addresses!'

Bill was pleased to discover that one of the new secretaries in his department was a good-looker and that she seemed to be giving him the eye. One night they both worked late, and he offered to take her for a meal — and soon one thing led to another and they ended up in bed at her place. By this time it was pretty late and Bill was worried about what his wife would say, so he rubbed some chalk into his hands, took a slug of whisky and made his way back home to face the music.

'And where do you think you've been?' were his wife's first words as he entered the house.

'If you must know, I've just had sex with the new secretary,' Bill muttered.

'Rubbish,' said his wife. 'You've got chalk all over you and you reek of whisky — you've been playing bloody snooker down at the club again!'

Did you read about the man who had some bad luck with the horses the other day? He put £200 on the Grand National winner each way. Unfortunately the bookie insisted that the horse had only gone *one* way.

Just this morning a table tennis player was taken to hospital after trying to jump the net at the end of the game ...

A famous fox-hunting man was at a party — and being lectured by a large lady who objected to the sport on grounds of its cruelty. For half an hour she went on about poor innocent foxes being torn apart by savage hounds, until finally the hunter's patience deserted him.

'Madam,' he cried, 'I can't agree with you. I have killed many foxes, but I have always spared them the ultimate cruelty — not one did I bore to death!'

An expert hunter took his young son out shooting for the day. Soon the man spotted a pheasant breaking cover, aimed, fired, and the bird fell with a thud at their feet. 'That was a waste of a shot,' said the boy. 'It would have died in the fall, anyway.'

Irish TV got into a terrible mix-up with their programme schedules the other day. They ordered ten episodes of Pot Black thinking that it was a cookery series.

A Chinese athlete recently set a terrific record for running over mountain, vallies, woods and swimming across lakes, but it was all in vain. He was recaptured.

50

The young boxer, facing his first fight, turned nervously to his opponent as they entered the ring. 'It's a long way from the changing rooms to here, isn't it?' he asked, trying to make conversation.

'It sure is,' said his massive opponent. 'But you don't have to worry about it. You won't be walking back.'

A young karate expert seemed set for a promising career in the Royal Marines. However things went wrong on his first day when he saluted — and knocked himself out.

'I've seen a wonderful game,' said the bowls umpire as he ushered the two players off the green, 'but that wasn't it.'

A pigeon-racer was having problems with his birds and wrote to the sport's board of control for advice.

'Dear Sir,' he wrote, 'I have difficulty with my pigeons. Every day I go up into the loft and find one or two of them lying stiff on the floor with their feet pointing up. Can you tell me what is wrong?'

He waited and waited for a reply, and eventually a letter came back from the board. 'Dear Sir,' it read, 'Your pigeons are dead.'

Did you hear about the failed sky-diver? He kept on missing the ground . . .

There was a sad story about an unlucky driver in the last Irish Grand Prix. He was two legs ahead and within sight of the finishing line when he clocked up 50,000 miles and had to make a pit stop to change his oil.

And then there was the tale of the poor Irish racing driver who had to stop 25 times in another Grand Prix. Once for petrol, twice for tyres, and 22 times to ask for directions.

An unfit man went to see the doctor and was told to take up jogging. 'You should run at least ten miles a day,' said the doctor. Two weeks later the man rang up the doctor to tell him he was feeling much better. 'That's excellent,' said the doctor. 'But you'd better come in and see me this afternoon so I can examine you properly.'

'But that's impossible,' said the man, 'I'm 150 miles away!'

A sportsman returned home after a lengthy tour of the world to find his wife pregnant. 'It can't be true,' he insisted to the doctor. 'I've been away for nearly twelve months!'

'I'm afraid,' said the doctor sympathetically, 'it's what we know in the profession as a grudge pregnancy.'

'What does that mean?'

'Put simply — someone had it in for you.'

The traditional Scottish sport of curling has had its fair share of dramatic moments. A player once fell through thawing ice as he was playing a vital shot. However, he managed to send the stone on its way before he fell in and as he sank he had made a near-perfect shot.

'Make sure that you put that on my headstone,' he called out as he disappeared under the icy waters.

A Jewish skier was enjoying a spell in the mountains one day when he got stuck in a drift. Soon the mountain rescue team were out looking for him. Night was beginning to close in as cries of 'Red Cross! Red Cross!' reached the freezing skier's ears.

'Oh, go away,' he yelled back to them. 'I already gave twice this year.'

Strong Stuff

*Although one of the first rules of speechmaking is not to use any material that will offend your audience, there are some occasions when a saucy joke will go down well — and you'll find some in this section. There's just one thing to remember. If **you** don't feel comfortable with the material don't use it, because your audience will sense your unhappiness. Be guided by your own taste and, if in doubt, leave it out.*

An ageing British soccer manager came out to the Middle East to do some coaching. When he arived he discovered that his home was to be a small all-male village in the centre of the desert. As he was exploring the place on his first day he came across a small hut in a quiet corner in which was kept a scruffy, ill-looking camel. He asked his companion what the camel was for and the man looked rather apologetic. 'Er,' he muttered, 'it's for the men when they get desperate. We're a long way from any women, you know.'

The soccer manager was horrified. 'That's the most disgusting thing I've ever heard,' he said, and stormed out.

The months passed and though the coaching went well the manager began to get very lonely. One day he could resist it no more. He went to the hut where the camel was kept, pulled up a stool and was just undoing his trousers when his earlier companion rushed in.

'No, no! You've made a big mistake,' he screamed. 'We use the camel for riding to the nearest brothel!'

The team's star footballer had mysteriously lost form only weeks before the cup final. The skipper after much questioning, learned that the player was depressed about his lack of sex life. This puzzled the captain because the striker was a fine athlete and very attractive to women. Again, after much probing, he found out that the player had a very strong foot fetish and that when it came to the crunch, few women were prepared to put up with his demands.

Desperate to satisfy his best player, the skipper dug deep into his own pocket and sent him to Soho where he would find someone who would tolerate him.

A week or two later a London doctor approached a nurse and said, 'It's amazing, Nurse Jenkins, but this job has its surprises even after 25 years. Only today I had two unique cases — a soccer player with VD of the big toe and a prostitute with athlete's foot of the fanny!'

There was a young soccer player who insisted on turning out for his club only a day before his wedding. Sure enough, within ten minutes of the kick-off he was kicked in the crotch and carried off to hospital. There surgeons carried out repairs and did him up in splints and bandages. The wedding itself went smoothly enough and the newlyweds arived at their honeymoon hotel. The bride, stunning but shy and wearing only a transparent negligee, lay down on the bed. 'Here I am, darling,' she whispered, 'untouched by man.'

'I can do even better than that,' said the bridegroom as he removed his pants. 'Look, mine hasn't even been unwrapped!'

Moira had been a golf widow to her Scots husband for many years — until one day he died and she became the real thing. His body was cremated and Moira took the ashes home with her in a box. In the solitude of her home, she opened the box and began talking to her husband in a way she had never been able to when he was alive. 'For years you kept me under control. You were too mean to buy me things for the house, you refused to let me play golf and you made unreasonable sexual demands on me.'

'Well,' she continued, 'now you've gone — and I'm going to have a new washing-machine, a dish-washer and carpets. And I've made friends with the president of the golf club and I'm going to play a round of golf every day.'

'And as,' she said, holding the box closer to her face, 'for that bloody blow job you were always pestering me for — *whoosh!*'

A bad golfer is like a bad lover — several strokes of foreplay, then he fails to enter the hole.

The Scottish rugby club president had just taken on the club's star player, a fly-half, at his firm. Several weeks went by, and someone asked the president how the player, who was having a brilliant season, was getting on at work. 'Well he's seduced my daughter, made love to my wife and touched up my secretary,' said the president.

'How awful — what are you going to do?'

'Don't worry,' said the president sternly. 'If I catch him fiddling the petty cash I'll be down on him like a ton of bricks!'

A powerful rugby forward seemed to lose his strength and had to be dropped from the side. Greatly perturbed at this loss of form, the team manager sent him to see a psychiatrist. The shrink asked the man about his dreams.

'Every night it's the same, Doctor,' he said. 'I dream I'm at Paddington with a wheelbarrow of concrete blocks and I have to push them to Maida Vale. I wake up knackered.'

The psychiatrist said that he could help. The player was to take a pill that he would prescribe. If he took it each night he would soon feel better. The player went home and took the pills and continued to have the same dream, except that before long the psychiatrist appeared and pushed the wheelbarrow to Maida Vale for him. So the rugby player woke up more refreshed than usual and pretty soon was able to regain his place in the team.

Naturally the whole club was impressed by this quick return to form and so when another player, a fly-half, began to play poorly they sent him to see the psychiatrist too. The fly-half explained his dreams. 'It's like this, Doctor. Each night I'm in this amazing bedroom when 12 lovely women walk in. They climb all over me, and they're so attractive that I make love to them all. When I wake up I'm exhausted!' Again the psychiatrist prescribed the pills, but this time the player's form got worse, not better. The skipper asked what was wrong. The fly-half said that now the shrink appeared and took six of the girls off his hands.

'Yes,' agreed the skipper. 'I suppose six girls are still rather a lot.'

'You don't understand,' said the player. 'When I get out-side, having finished with the girls, I find some bugger's left a wheelbarrow full of bricks that I have to wheel all the way to Maida Vale!'

A young housewife was confessing her secrets to a good friend. 'Some very odd things have been happening lately. On Tuesday this young athlete who was jogging past the house knocked on the door and asked, 'Is your husband Jack in?' I said no, so this chap grabbed me, took me upstairs and made love to me for hours.'

'On Wednesday it was the same thing. He knocked on the door, asked if Jack was in and when I said no, took me upstairs again. Yesterday, exactly the same — "Is Jack in?" No, I say, so we go upstairs and make love all morning. There's just one thing I don't understand.'

'What's that?' asked the amazed friend.

'What on earth does he want with our Jack?'

A Scottish athlete travelled over to Athens for a major championship and one evening went to a brothel. He asked for one of the girls in particular, had sex, then gave her £200. The next evening he was back again for a repeat performance with the same girl and for the same sum. For two more nights he repeated the routine. On the fourth night the girl, who had thoroughly enjoyed her encounters with him, begged him to return the next night.

'I can't,' said the Scot. 'My events have ended and I must go back to Glasgow. Anyway, I know your uncle there. He gave me £800 to give to you.'

Three Olympic athletes, all fine specimens of young manhood, were boasting about their prowess in bed. The German said he made love to his wife once every hour, on the hour, making eight or nine times a night. The others asked what his wife said to him in the morning.

'Ah, she says it was wunderbar, wunderbar!'

Next the Frenchman described how he made love to his mistress. 'Many times I make love to her. Then I rest and do it again and again. Perhaps twenty times in one night,' he boasted. The other two asked what she said to him in the morning.

'She says I am magnifique, simply magnifique.'

Finally it was the turn of the Englishman to describe how he made love to his wife. 'I just do it once,' he said simply.

'Once?' the other two cried in unison. 'What does your wife say in the morning?'

'I think you'd better get off now and give us both a rest.'

One morning a young athlete was up in court for stealing a bike. The magistrates told him to describe what happened.

'Well, your worships,' he began, 'I was jogging through the woods when this pretty young girl came up on a bike and persuaded me to sit down with her. I wasn't tired, but I did so. Then she took off her blouse, though it wasn't very warm, then she said, "Kiss me," so I did.'

'And then?' the magistrate asked.

'Then she lifted up her skirt and told me I could have anything I wanted.'

'And then?' asked the magistrate.

'So I took her bike.'

Sporting Life

Sporting stories say a great deal about the human condition, and you're bound to find one in this collection that will illustrate your speech perfectly. After all, if life is a game of cricket, as Lord Dorset said in 1777, it's no wonder that the world's a mess. How many people do you know who know the rules of cricket?

The legendary Everton forward Dixie Dean was a formidable header of the ball. Once he was walking down a street on the day of the big local derby when he saw the Liverpool goalie on the other side of the road. Out of courtesy Dean nodded his head to him — and legend has it that the goalie, out of habit, dived to make the 'save' . . . straight through the window of a shop.

In the days when the two lower soccer divisions were divided regionally into North and South, Liverpool had just been relegated into Division Two and were having a bad season. During one game their centre forward rose to head the ball but instead gave his head a nasty smack on the cross bar. He was immediately carried off and taken to the Royal Northern Hospital. When the striker eventually came round he was disorientated and called out to the nurse, 'Where the hell am I?'

'It's okay,' she replied comfortingly, 'you're in the Northern.'

'Blimey,' said the concussed footballer, 'we weren't long in the Second, were we?'

The football club chairman made a morale-boosting visit to his team, who had not been doing too well of late. As he arrived in the changing rooms he was peeved to find only four players and a ball-boy waiting to hear him. He turned on the manager who was cowering behind him. 'Did you tell them all that I was coming?' he asked fiercely.

'Oh no,' said the manager in a whisper. 'Someone must have leaked it.'

Ipswich Town had just beaten Arsenal in breathtaking style in the FA Cup final. The club's president, Lady Blanche Cobbold, was asked by an official if she wanted to go and meet the guest of honour — Mrs Thatcher.

'Frankly,' replied Lady Cobbold, 'I'd much rather have a gin and tonic.'

Bill Shankley, the former Liverpool manager, was utterly dedicated to football. He was once asked by an impertinent journalist if it was true that he had taken his wife to see a reserve team match as a wedding anniversary treat.

'It's not true at all,' said Shankley vehemently. 'That's a lie.' Then he paused and added. 'It was her birthday.'

The secretary of an Irish football club asked his wife to take a presentation tankard to the engravers and dictated the inscription to her. She wrote it down and handed it over with the tankard. Unfortunately the inscription had been written on a shopping list and the tankard was returned bearing the words 'One bottle of shoe cleaner and a pair of white laces.'

Few journalists have ever got the better of Bill Shankley. His team was once beaten 5-1 in a European cup match. A cocky reporter put it to Shanks that he had to admit his team had been well and truly smashed this time.

Shankley turned on the young man. 'We canna play football against defensive teams,' he said. And he meant it.

After his team's famous and unexpected win over arch-rivals Manchester United in 1968, Colin Bell, the Manchester City player, was asked how he felt.

'Chuffed,' came the simple reply.

The newspaper man persisted. 'Look, this was a fantastic victory and you played a blinder. How do you really feel?'

Bell paused and then said quietly, 'Very chuffed.'

Fred, an ageing football fan, finally achieved his ambition of going to Wembley to see his team play in the Cup Final. He was very distressed to see that the two seats next to him were empty only minutes before kick-off. Eventually, seconds before the start, a man raced up and took one of the seats.

Fred took no time in engaging him in conversation. 'I think it's scandalous,' he told his new companion. 'I've tried for tickets in the past and never got one, and what do I find when I eventually get here but an empty seat next to me.'

'I agree with you entirely,' said his neighbour. 'The truth is that the other seat was for my wife, who sadly died three days ago.'

Fred was only slightly taken aback. 'Well, you could have given the ticket away to a friend or relative.'

'No chance,' said his neighbour. 'They're an unsporting family. They've all gone to the funeral instead.'

There was once on the golf circuit an explosive young player called Tommy 'Thunder' Bolt. Although he was usually a happy guy, he was liable to explode if things went wrong on the links. People took bets not on how many shots he'd take but how many clubs he'd have left when he finished a round. He once came to the final hole and asked his young caddie what club was needed for a difficult tee shot. 'A six-iron,' replied the caddie.

'What?' exploded Bolt, 'A six-iron? But it's more than 200 yards to the flag! How can you say it's a six-iron?'

'Because that's all that's left in the bag,' sighed the caddie.

An Australian golfer mis-hit his tee shot and, cursing, went to fetch it from the river. Imagine his surprise when he found the ball had hit and killed a two-pound fish! The lucky golfer took it home and had the fish for his lunch.

The foxy Argentinian golfer Roberto de Vicenzo fooled his Australian companion Noel Ratcliffe as they played a practice round before the British Open. They were just about to tee-off on one hole, a dog-leg with a massive row of trees in the corner when de Vicenzo said, 'When I was your age, I used to hit the ball over those trees.' Naturally Ratcliffe could not resist the challenge and tried to smash the ball over the top of them. But he didn't make it and drove right into the thicket.

'But then,' finished the wily old pro, 'those trees had only just been planted.'

Australian cricket commentator Alan McGilvray, once put his foot in it when he described the fate of Aussie test batsman Kim Hughes. 'It's been a weekend of delight and disappointment for Hughes,' said McGilvray to millions of listeners. 'His wife presented him with twins yesterday . . . and a duck today.'

W.G. Grace, the master batsman, was not one to keep quiet about his crowd-pulling potential. Playing on a tour of Australia, he faced a young bowler from a local district team. Amazingly, the very first ball beat his guard and knocked over the stumps. Bowler and fielders celebrated. However, Grace stayed his ground and replaced the bails.

'I never could play the practice ball,' he said casually, taking guard. Not surprisingly the bowler was not prepared to leave the matter there and demanded that Grace leave the crease.

'Now look here,' retorted the master, 'these people have paid to see me bat, not you bowl — so let's get on with it!'

The Yorkshire spinner Hedley Verity, normally a difficult bowler to hit, was once collared by a big South African hitter. The batsman clobbered him for two sixes and three fours in one over. At the end of it one of Verity's colleagues came over to him. 'It's okay, Hedley,' said the player. 'Reckon you've got him in two minds.'

'How do you mean, in two minds?' puzzled the spinner.

'He doesn't know whether to hit you for four or six.'

At one time in cricket the bowling team could claim a new ball when 100 runs were on the board instead of after a set number of overs. Once, an Australian touring team in India were being introduced to important local dignitaries. 'This is the Maharajah of this area,' said the team manager as he introduced him to the side. 'He is one of the wealthiest men in the world — and he also has 199 wives.'

'Crikey,' remarked one of the players. 'One more and he'd need a new ball.'

That tough cricketer Brian Close was fielding close to the wicket at short leg when the batsman produced a full-blooded pull shot and the ball hit the fielder hard on the side of this face. Amazingly it flew straight up in the air and the batsman was caught at slip.

'My God,' said a worried fielder going to check up on Close. 'What would have happened if he'd hit you right between the eyes?'

'In that case,' growled Close, 'the bugger would have been caught at cover.'

John Wisden, the founder of the famed cricketer's almanack and no mean cricketer, was once sailing across the Atlantic as part of a tour. A furious gale blew up and the seas were running very high. Turning to a colleague he said, 'What this pitch needs is ten minutes with a heavy roller.'

During the festival week of cricket at Weston-Super-Mare, the visiting team, Surrey, stayed at a large local hotel. The Surrey skipper, Percy Fender, pointed out to the management that there wasn't 'enough room to swing a cat, in his bedroom. 'I'm very sorry, sir,' said the manager. 'I didn't realise you'd come to Weston for the cat-swinging.'

The prolific Hampshire batsman Phil Mead found a novel way of getting out. His captain, Lord Tennyson, relying on Mead to occupy the crease, would take a leisurely bath in the pavilion while his team batted. He would get dressed and put on his pads before summoning a Post Office messenger boy to dictate a message.

A few minutes later a telegram would be hurried out to the middle with an 'urgent message' for one of the batsman. It would simply read, 'Mead. Get out at once. Tennyson.'

Those two great cricketing stalwarts Bomber Wells and Sam Cook were batting for Gloucestershire when they made an almighty mess of going for a run.

'Call, Bomber!' cried Sam.

'Heads!' replied his companion.

Many forget that W.G. Grace was a respected doctor besides being a cricketing legend. One day a timid man turned up at the surgery and asked, 'Is the doctor in?'

'Of course he's in,' snapped the assistant. 'He's been batting since Monday.'

The Duke personally organised his side's annual circet match with a neighbouring village team. The game was played at his own grounds and took place in perfect surroundings. The Duke had just come in to bat when his partner, wanting to give his Lordship a chance, called for a quick single. Alas, half-way down the pitch the Duke tripped and fell, leaving him stranded helpless and yards from the crease.

The opposing wicket keeper whipped off the bails and loudly appealed, 'Howzat?' The umpire was the Duke's own butler, drafted in as a late replacement. Naturally the butler was in something of a dilemma and paused to give thought about what to do. Eventually, after what seemed an age, he lifted himself up to his full height and grandly declared, 'His Lordship is not in.'

Fred Price, the Middlesex wicket keeper, had just taken a record seven catches in one innings. A woman approached him afterwards in the bar and said, 'Oh, Mr Price, I was so excited by your wicket keeping today I nearly fell out of the balcony.'

'And had you done so, madam,' said Fred, 'on today's form I'd have caught you!'

The Fijians, entertaining rugby players, were often amused by the interest their 'humble' origins caused. On the 1970 tour of Britain a novice journalist asked one of the massive Fijian forwards how they celebrated after a game in their country. 'The winners eat the losers,' he replied.

Players on the 1980 Lions tour of South Africa were doubtless encouraged by this piece of advice from their coach, Noel Murphy, before a game. 'Right, lads,' he said, 'I want 80 per cent concentration for 100 minutes.'

The Blantyre rugby club from Malawi were about to make a tour to Mauritius when the secretary of the rugby club in that country sent an urgent telegram. 'Please bring your own ball,' it read. 'We have lost ours.'

Blackheath player Arnold Alcock was surprised to receive a letter asking him to play for England against South Africa in a rugby international in 1906. After all, even by his own admission Alcock was just an ordinary club player. He turned up on the day, but when he did so the team secretary realised he'd made a ghastly mistake. The letter *should* have been sent to Andrew Slocock. However, it was too late to change things, so Alcock got his cap — but was never picked again!

An All Black full-back was taking part in a charity rugby match when he caught the ball from a clearance, ran through a gap in the defence and scored with a flourish under the posts. The only problem was that he was *supposed* to be the referee!

On their 1982 tour of the States, England's three-quarters were developing a good movement in the middle of the field when to their amazement the referee blew his whistle and halted the game. He explained to the baffled players that the game was being sponsored by a TV station and therefore he had to stop for commercial breaks. 'I wore a bleeper,' he said. 'Three bleeps and I had to stop for precisely one minute.'

In 1968 a student revolt broke out in Paris and for one week the French capital was cut off from the outside world. The phones were cut off and the airports were closed. By chance at this time an English rugby team were visiting Paris for a brief tour and one journalist, a dour northern sportswriter called Fred, was with them.

Oblivious of all the momentous events going on around him, Fred spent all day trying to phone his office. Finally, with minutes to spare before his deadline, he managed to get a line through to his northern newspaper office. His call caused an incredible stir and he was passed straight through to the news editor.

'What the hell's going on over there?' asked the editor. 'Do you realise you're the only journalist who's been able to get through to us? What's happening?'

The bemused Fred told him that some strange things had been happening. 'A tank's just come through the wall of the hotel as I'm speaking to you,' he reported.

'This is brilliant,' said the news editor excitedly, foreseeing all kinds of exclusives. 'I'm going to put you straight through to a copy typist. Give us all you've got, Fred.'

So Fred was passed over to the copy department while the editor planned how to handle the world scoop. Slightly baffled, Fred began to dictate his copy over the phone. 'Eric Jenkinson, the Widnes forward, is to have a fitness test on his suspect left knee . . .'

A couple of hundred words later and Fred put down the phone, his job well done, and wandered off happily to look for a drink.

And meanwhile the revolution went on all round him . . .

Welshman Keith Jarrett had a memorable day in 1967 when, aged only 19 and on his international debut, he scored 19 points to help the Welsh side defeat the English at Cardiff by 34-21.

After the celebrations Jarrett had to catch a bus to Newport where he lived. Unfortunately when he got to the bus station the last bus had gone and it was an eight-mile walk to Newport. Luckily a driver who was knocking off recognised Jarrett from his sterling deeds at the Arms Park that day and offered him a lift in a bus. As they moved off an inspector stopped them. 'What are you doing?' he asked the driver.

'I'm taking Mr Jarrett home — he scored 19 points against England.' The inspector checked, recognised Jarrett and said to the driver, 'You fool! Go and get a double decker — the lad might want to smoke!'

At a charity gala athlete Alan Pascoe was talking to Prince Philip about a stomach injury he had sustained hurdling. 'I don't know what's wrong with you athletes,' said Prince Philip. 'You get more injuries than my bloody horses.'

67

'Perhaps you ought to put me in touch with a vet,' said the hurdler.

'If I did that, you'd end up in the knacker's yard!'

At the end of the third round boxer Max Baer returned to his corner after another mauling from Joe Louis. His corner-man, Jack Dempsey, greeted him. 'Keep going, you're doing fine. The other guy hasn't even hit you yet.'

'In that case,' mumbled Baer through swollen, blood-stained lips, 'you'd better keep an eye on the referee next round, cause some guy is sure beating the hell out of me.'

The true story is told of when an Irish farmer bet one hundred pounds with a bookie called Finnegan on a horse at 7-1. The animal duly cantered in to pass the post first and the farmer, no lover of bookies, went to collect his £700. As he did so he was heard to repeat several times, 'You've heard of Finnegan's Wake, well this is your wake, Finnegan.'

That brilliant jockey Lester Piggott was known to put his hardness of hearing to good effect. He was accosted by a down-and-out fan, who appealed for assistance one day. 'Please,' said the old man feebly, 'just a couple of quid for a life-long fan,' Lester seemed not to hear and continued on his way, but the man was persistent. 'Please, Mr Piggott,' he hollered in his ear, 'just a fiver for an old and loyal fan.'

'What's that?' said Lester. 'Just now it was only a couple of quid!'

There are strict rules about the kind of clothing that darts players may wear at major competitions where television cameras are present — and jeans are not allowed. One year this caused quite a stir at the British Open. A player was about to begin playing in the quarter finals wearing jeans when he was dragged off the stage by two large officials, taken out of view of the TV cameras, debagged — and given another more acceptable pair of trousers to wear!

Darts star John Lowe strolled into the bar after losing a semi-final in an important championship. 'I want nineteen brandies, a double vodka and a whisky,' he called to the barman. 'All in the same glass.'

Tennis ace Ilie Nastasie admitted he had failed to report that his American Express card had gone missing. As he put it, 'Whoever stole it is bound to be spending less than my wife.'

An Australian snooker player decided to invent a new shot, to be called after him, and had himself suspended upside down over the table with helium balloons attached to his wrists and his legs fastened to the rafters of the building. Sadly his arrangements went wrong and while making his shot he fell head-first onto the table and died.

Sporting Talk

In this section of sporting quotes you'll find the famous and the not-so-famous — words of unforgettable wisdom and appalling slips of the tongue that sports commentators have been hoping we'll all forget!

Players who lose are worse than bank robbers.

Bill Shankley

I've got no time for shirkers. I want a man who'll go through a wall of fire, break a leg, and still come out shooting for goal.

Bill Shankley

All a manager had to do is keep 11 players happy — the 11 in the reserves. The first team are happy because they're the first team.

Rodney Marsh

There are only two basic situations in football — either you have the ball or you haven't.

Ron Greenwood

Our problem is that we have tried to score too many goals.

Gordon Lee, manager of Everton

It's those buggers on the sports pages I hate most.

Brian Clough

Brains? There's a lot of players who think manual labour is the Spanish president.

Tommy Docherty

I'd give my right arm to get back into the England team.

Peter Shilton, goalkeeper

For those of you watching in black and white, Spurs are in the all-yellow strip.

John Motson, sports commentator

Remeber now, postcards only, please. The winner will be the first one opened.

Brian Moore, announcing a soccer quiz

I'm convinced that the greatest contribution that Britain has made to the national life in Uruguay was teaching people football.

Prince Philip

I have this book with players' names in it. If I get the chance to do them I will. I'll make them suffer before I pack it in. If I can kick them four yards over the touchline I will.

Jack Charlton

Asked if he would name his side for that night's match against Milan, *Bill Shankley* said: 'I'm not going to give any secrets like that to Milan. If I had my way I wouldn't even tell them the time of the kick-off.'

The rules are very simple, basically it is this; if it moves, kick it. If it doesn't move, kick it till it does.

US soccer promoter Phil Woosnam, on suggestions that the Americans might find the rules of soccer difficult.

Professionalism, if you like, is not having sex on Thursdays and Fridays.

Don Revie

Say nowt, win it, then talk your head off.
Brian Clough on how to manage the media

If you watch a game, it's fun. If you play it, it's recreation. If you work at it, it's golf.

Bob Hope

Someone sent a shilling towards W.G. Grace's testimonial with a note that said: 'It's not in support of cricket, but as an earnest protest against golf.'

Golf is so popular simply because it's the best game in the world at which to be bad.

A.A. Milne

All I've got against golf is that it takes you so far from the clubhouse.

Eric Linklater

If a woman can walk she can play golf.

Louise Suggs

The least things upset him on the links. He missed short putts because of the uproar of butterflies in adjoining meadows.

P.G. Wodehouse

Golf — a good walk spoiled.

Mark Twain

Statistics indicate that, as a result of overwork, modern executives are dropping like flies on the nation's golf courses.

Ira Wallach

I am sure that the Almighty never intended that cricket should be played in anything but glorious sunshine, especially if the wicket was doing a bit.

Ray Illingworth

Try explaining cricket to an intelligent foreigner. It is far harder than trying to explain Chomsky's generational grammar.

Lord Snow

If they don't cooperate they'll walk straight into a meat mangle.

Kerry Packer on the Australian Cricket Board

It won't take much work to get me psyched up to hating anyone.

Jeff Thomson

I have always imagined cricket as a game invented by roughnecks in a moment of idleness by casually throwing an unexploded bomb at one another. The game was observed by some officer with a twisted and ingenious mind who devoted his life to inventing impossible rules for it.

Peter Ustinov

Personally I have always looked on cricket as organised loafing.

William Temple (later Archbishop of Canterbury)

It's a funny kind of month, October. For the really keen cricket fan it's when you discover your wife left you in May.

Dennis Norden

What is life but a game of cricket?

Duke of Dorset

A cricketer — a creature very nearly as stupid as a dog.

Bernard Levin

I would have got a better mention in Pravda.

Kerry Packer, on his bad press

I have nightmares about having to become an umpire.

John Snow

One fact seems sure;
That, while the Church approves, Lord's will endure.

Siegfried Sassoon

He played his cricket on the heath,
The pitch was full of bumps:
A fast ball hit him in the teeth —
The dentist drew the stumps.

Anon

I tend to believe that cricket is the greatest thing that God ever created on earth.

Harold Pinter

Rugby is a beastly game played by gentlemen; soccer is a gentlemen's game played by beasts; and American football is a beastly game played by beasts.

Henry Bahia

Fishing, with me, has always been an excuse to drink in the daytime.

Jimmy Cannon, sportswriter

If you want to be happy for a day, get drunk.
If you want to be happy for a week, get married.
But if you want to be happy for life, go fishing.

Anon

Angling — I can only compare it to a stick and a string with a worm at one end and a fool at the other.

Dr Johnson

All men are equal before fish.

Herbert Hoover, US president

Fishing is a delusion entirely surrounded by liars in old clothes.

Don Marquis

Angling — the name given to fishing by those people who can't fish.

Stephen Leacock

A good darts player who can count can always beat a brilliant player who can't.

Leighton Rees

Boxing is showbusines with blood.

David Belasco, US impresario

I must be the greatest — am I immortal too?
And ... I'm not an ordinary mortal, I'm bigger than the sport itself. And ... I don't believe all the stuff I say.

Muhammed Ali

Boxing is not a sport, it is a criminal activity.

Prof. Ernst Johl

Boxing is the best and most individual lifestyle you can have in society without being a criminal.

Randy Neumann, US boxer

Boxing is sort of like jazz. The better it is the fewer people can understand it.

George Foreman

A lot of boxing promoters couldn't match the cheeks of their own backsides.

Mickey Duff, entrepreneur and promoter

You're damn right I know where I am — I'm in Madison Square Gardens getting beaten up!
Willie Pastrano, boxer, when knocked down in the ring and asked by the referee if he knew where he was

Clay can't insult me. I'm too ignorant.
Brian London, boxer

I'm only a prawn in this game.
Brian London

If you hadn't been there it wouldn't have been much of a fight.
Harry Carpenter to Ken Norton after a bout

I lost it by default, not de punch.
John Conteh, stripped of his title

My plans usually work. If they don't I resort to brutality.
George Foreman

My first priority is to finish racing above rather than beneath the ground.
James Hunt

In my sport (motor racing) the quick are often listed among the dead.
Jackie Stewart

It is necessary to relax your muscles when you can. Relaxing your brain is fatal.
Sterling Moss

To play billiards well is a sign of misspent youth.
Herbert Spencer

There's more tension and electrification in snooker as a sport than in any other kind, even motor-racing.

John Pulman, snooker champion

If someone died in the ring, they'd say it was faked.

US professional wrestler

The Americas Cup is as exciting as watching grass grow.

US sportswriter

It's Oxford! No, it's Cambridge. I can't see. It's Oxford. No ... well, one of them must be winning.

John Snagge commentating on 1954 Boat Race

The fascination of shooting as a sport depends almost wholly on whether you are on the right or wrong end of the gun.

P.G. Wodehouse

The English country gentleman galloping after a fox — the unspeakable in pursuit of the uneatable.

Oscar Wilde

Pro football is like nuclear warfare. There are no winners, only survivors.

Frank Gifford

I never did say that you can't be a nice guy and win. I said that if I was playing third base and my mother rounded third with a winning run I'd trip her up.

Leo Durocher, US baseball manager

I gave George Allen unlimited patience and he exhausted it.

US team owner on firing his coach

I sometimes get birthday cards from fans. But it's often the same message — they hope it's my last.

Al Norman, US baseball umpire

Asked whether he preferred astroturf to grass, *Joe Namath*, US pro footballer, said: 'I don't know. I never smoked astroturf.'

When I was 40 my doctor advised me that a man in his forties should not play tennis. I heeded his advice carefully and could hardly wait until I reached 50 to start again.

Hugo Black

Running for money doesn't make you run fast. It makes you run first.

Ben Jipcho, Kenyan runner

Look at that tremendous flexibility of the ankles. They really are an extension of the legs.

Ron Pickering, sports commentator

This game is passionate enough without money.

Richard Rodgers, composer and croquet player

What I like best about bullfighting is the big money and small bulls.

Spanish matador

To win is everything. To be second is even worse than being secondary.

David Broome

To win is worthless if you don't get paid for it.

Reggie Jackson, US sportsman

Winning is not everything. It's the only thing.

Vince Lombardi, US pro football coach

Winners aren't popular. Losers often are.

Virginia Wade

The problem with good losers is they get into the habit of losing.

Knute Rochne, US pro football coach

Serious sport has nothing to do with fair play.

George Orwell

As I understand it, sport is hard work for which you do not get paid.

Irvine S. Cole

If you are fit, you don't need it. If you aren't, you shouldn't risk it.

Henry Fonda on exercise

Sporting Feats

Sport seems to have more than its fair share of amazing facts and bizarre feats, so make your audience laugh with some of these incredible snippets of information. Believe it or not, they're all true!

Oxbarn Social Club, a football side from Wolverhampton, had an unnerving experience when they went on a brief tour of Germany in 1973. They arrived in the city of Mainz where, to their surprise, they were booked to play in a large stadium. Even odder, and very flattering, they heard rumours that the opposition were on an £80 per man bonus to beat them. These Germans certainly take the game seriously, they thought.

On the day of the game there were queues of fans outside the stadium — and when the match started it was a massacre. The amused crowd cheered each time the English side managed to cross the half-way line, which wasn't often. The final result was 21-0 to the Germans.

Club secretary Ron Parker explained later how the posters outside the ground had revealed the extent of the confusion. They read SVW Mainz V Wolverhampton Wanderers.

Fans at Sicilian football match were outraged when the referee sent off a local player during a heated incident. One, particularly incensed, rushed home and fetched a shotgun. He then fired several warning shots in the air and pointed the gun at the ref while he demanded the player be reinstated. Not having any wish to die, the referee agreed. Unfortunately the visiting side's goalie was so upset by the gun-toting display and the fact that the fan was still waving the weapon in his direction, that he tactfully let in seven goals.

The great footballer Pele was probably the only player in history to stop a war. Both sides agreed on a truce during the Biafran conflict so that they could watch the genius play on his African tour.

A resourceful referee once managed to get his own back on a hostile crowd and players in that graveyard of sports officials, Italy. The soccer official, Senor Benedetti, disallowed two penalties for the home side and was chased through the streets by an angry mob. Fortunately he found sanctuary in a quiet restaurant. He was just about to tuck into a meal when the owner, a football fan, recognised him and threw him out.

The ref took his revenge by phoning the restaurant in a disguised voice, claiming to be the manager of the home side and saying that he was bringing the whole team there in an hour. He then rang the team manager, pretending to be the restaurant owner, and invited the team to come round for a cheap meal to compensate for being robbed in the match. The team arrived and ate and drank enormous amounts. When they were presented with the bill there was a fracas which resulted in the team manager being imprisoned . . .

It was the rowdiness of the adults and not the players that led to the cancellation of Northamptonshire Scout troop matches in 1977. During the finals of the tournament a gang of parents began to fight each other at the touchline and two brawling mothers chased a linesman across the pitch.

Imposing a six-year ban on Scout football, the Scout District Commissioner said: 'I have blown the whistle for the last time.'

Lady golfer Mrs Bobby Pritchard faced a novel problem one morning as she played a round at her local course in Rhodesia. Her ball had settled among the coils of a ten-foot long python. Wisely deciding not to rush the shot, and too honest just to use another ball, she consulted the club secretary. His ruling was authoritative — shoot the creature and then play the stroke. And this she did.

An Australian golf course near Darwin was so prone to invasion by local wildlife that the club was compelled to introduce a new rule. It read: 'Where a hawk, lizard, crocodile, snake or wallaby takes the ball, another shall be dropped.'

On an American golf course near Washington there was a problem one year with a black bear on the fairway. New rules were accordingly drafted, which ran as follows. 'If a ball is picked up by a bear, people may replace and take one penalty stroke. If the player gets the ball back from the bear, take an automatic par for hole.'

Perhaps the most unusual reason ever for stopping a cricket match occurred in Fiji some years ago. Heavy rain had prevented any play, but when the sun came out the players turned up for a practice game . . . only to find the entire pitch covered by little green frogs which had taken advantage of the moisture to pop up from the turf.

In 1911 Nottingham cricketer Ted Alletson scored the fastest sustained innings ever in the first-class game — 189 in just 90 minutes. Remarkably, the last 142 of these came in only 40 minutes! During his savage knock he lost five balls as he hit them past the boundaries of the Hove ground. But even more incredibly, this was Alletson's first and only century and after failing to score more than 11 in subsequent innings he was eventually dropped.

The following appeared on a cricket scoreboard in Australia in 1979. Lillee caught Willey bowled Dilley 19.

In 1949 a powerful batsman hit a six into a field and killed a goose.

In Adelaide during a Test match a more formidable bird, a large seagull, swooped onto the field to save England two runs from an Australian shot. The ball hit the bird and stopped dead — and the gull was treated for shock and a leg injury.

W.G. Grace once hit a ball 37 miles — quite a feat, even for him. It happened when he was playing at Hull and smashed a ball into a passing railway truck. Its next stop was Leeds!

A determined Lancashire angler was found by a Rochdale policeman fishing through the grating of a drain. 'I'm fighting for the right of anyone to fish where they like,' he explained. The court nevertheless fined him £15 for obstruction.

A Norfolk fisherman caught a 12-pound cod whose stomach contained a packet of salt and vinegar flavour crisps.

Angler Mr E. Curry was doubtless disappointed when, in a fishing competition at Walton-on-the-Naze, he caught only one fish, a measly 9oz flounder. But he needn't have worried because the fish was still enough to win. None of the other anglers caught a thing.

After five hours of dedicated fishing the 200 competitors in the 1972 National Ambulanceman's Championship were slightly baffled that no one, not one person, had caught a single fish. Just then a local man walked past and told them why. 'Didn't you know that the local authority drained that stretch of water three weeks ago — they've only just refilled it!'

Opponents of one Yugoslavian rugby team were disconcerted to find themselves playing against a second row called Arsenic and a prop called Panic!

Radford School's rugby team once beat their opponents from Hills Court 200-0, including 38 tries.

On one remarkable rugby occasion in Argentina in 1920 all 30 players and the entire crowd of 2,500 were arrested and jailed by the police. Apparently the authorities thought that it was some kind of political gathering . . .

In 1984 an Abertillery rugby player was helped off the pitch at the end of the game — suffering from exposure.

During an Olympic bout a young boxer had his gumshield knocked out. He immediately knelt down and began to scramble around on his hands and knees to pick it up in his boxing-glove — not an easy task.

    As he did so the referee began counting, and ten seconds later counted the unfortunate boxer out!

A large man came out of an American bank one day carrying an official-looking bag. Just then another man pulled a knife on him and told him to hand over the bag. The big man did so — and the weight of $400 in coins knocked the attacker backwards. As he stumbled and fell the big chap, otherwise known as heavyweight boxing champ Alex Venettis, knocked him out cold with a right hook.

At the 1972 Olympics, held in Germany, a British kayak pair got stuck in the rapids during the slalom event. They were trapped upside down in the water against a rock. 'I don't wish to appear pessimistic,' said the BBC commentator, 'but I sense our medal chances are slipping away.' Having righted themselves, one of the men discovered that he had lost his watch during the mishap. The entire artificial course was drained to look for it!

In 1912 a Japanese runner named Shizo Kanakuni stopped during the marathon to ask for a cool drink. Finding himself still some miles from the finishing line in Stockholm, Kanakuni decided he had had enough and took a tram back to the Swedish capital. Then, without telling anyone, he took a boat back to Japan. His disappearance remained a mystery until 1963, when a Swedish reporter traced the runner back to Japan and persuaded him to return to the spot where he had quit the marathon. So finally Kanakuni finished the race he had started — and it only took him 50 years!

Surinam only sent one athlete to the 1960 Rome Olympics, an 800 metre runner. After his arrival by plane in Italy he was natually tired and decided to take a nap. He slept right through the morning, rose and took a light meal, then made his way to the stadium — only to discover that the event was over.

Three US athletes were watching afternoon television at the Munich Olympics in 1972 when, to their horror, their second round 100m sprint was announced. They checked the times and found that they had confused 15.00 hours with 5 p.m. All three dashed to the stadium but only one made it on time. He at least had the satisfaction of winning the silver medal.

The official starter for the sprints at the 1904 Olympics at St Louis, Missouri, was so annoyed at three false starts in one race that he punished the four runners by making them run an extra metre. The winner, Archie Hahn, now holds a unique record — the 201m won in 21.6 seconds.

Just four men took part in the 400m Olympic finals held in London in 1908, one Briton and three Americans. As they came round the bend heading for home, one of the Americans appeared to impede the Briton, Lieutenant Wyndham Halswelle, and to the astonishment of all a British official named Dr Badger ran to the finishing line and ordered the judge to cut the tape. This meant that the race was void and a re-run was ordered, with the offending American excluded. So furious were the other two American runners that they refused to participate — so Halswelle ran on his own . . . and naturally he won.

An American runner named Billy Jones made athletics history when in 1955 he ran the 100 yards in 9.0 seconds dead. The crowd were ecstatic and Jones himself was overjoyed until officials checked the track — and found that it was only 90 yards long.

A Swedish runner, Dan Waern, caused controversy in the sport when questions were asked about the true nature of his supposedly amateur status. His own athletics board opted to back him, but eventually he was suspended and took the only course left open to him — and turned professional. His first exhibition race in Sweden attracted a large and expectant crowd. They were not disappointed. Waern had decided to run 1,000m against a team of schoolgirls and a team of schoolboys. The race began and after a tough battle the newly-professional athlete managed to out-run the girls. Alas, however, the schoolboys beat him by an entire lap.

Although he had come all the way from Guinea Bissau in Africa, a long-distance runner from the country refused point blank to take part in the 3,000m steeplechase at the Moscow Olympics. It seemed that the problem concerned the water jump.

'You don't just jump into water in Guinea Bissau,' he explained. 'There might be crocodiles!'

Pity the poor Russian oarsman who, in 1956, won the single sculls in the Melbourne Olympics. So excited was he at getting the gold that he threw the medal high into the air — and down it plunged into the nearby lake, never to be seen again. The authorities later gave him a duplicate medal.

In 1980 an official at a haggis-throwing competition in Scotland was measuring a throw when he was hit on the head by a flying haggis and knocked out.

A north Rhodesian bar was full of men playing darts and drinking, listening to the heavy rain outside. Suddenly one of the men froze as he saw a deadly puff adder slithering across the floor towards him. Things looked dangerous — then Colin Browne, the local darts champion gave a flick of the wrist and pinned the snake to the floor with a single dart. Naturally everyone was much relieved, except for Browne; rules being rules, he lost his match for missing the board.

An American football coach was ordered to stop chewing heads off frogs in front of his young players in his pre-match pep talk. He complained, saying that the kids loved it.

A tennis competition was held up by heavy rain in Calcutta in 1975 — a table tennis competition. Thieves had stolen the lead from the roof and the rain poured in and onto the tables.

Frisbee thrower Julius T Nachazel went into the woods at Eagle Harbour in California to retrieve his frisbee — and was never seen again. To this day no one knows what happened to him. His sad fate caught the imagination of fellow frisbee enthusiasts and now there is a championship named after him.

The Front Line

The best way to start your speech is with a quick joke or quote that will break the ice and establish contact between you and your audience — and for this a one-liner is ideal. When you tell a one-line joke don't labour it too hard, just drop it casually into your speech and leave it to the audience to find the humour. They'll be flattered to think that you can afford to risk wasting lines on them!

Did you hear about the Division Four football manager who was taken to hospital suffering from a bad side?

Our local football team was so bad that when they won a corner they took a lap of honour.

Another football team knew they shouldn't have appointed a goalkeeper called Cinderella. He kept missing the ball.

Why did the Irish football team play a blushing young virgin as goalkeeper? They knew she wouldn't let one in all season.

Graffiti: Joe Jordan kicks the parts other beers don't reach. Liverpool are magic — Everton are tragic.

Spurs striker Garth Crooks once announced to the press, 'The goal surprised many people, least of all myself.'

A soccer commentator talking about Ian Rush said: 'Deadly ten times out of ten — but that wasn't one of them.'

The local football manager is teaching his side speedway. He reckons that's the only way they'll reach Wembley.

Did you hear about the man who thought that Sheffield Wednesday was the beginning of Lent?

Jesus may save — but Shilton is better.

The local paper recently reported on a man who gave up golf to become a catholic. He said the rules were easier to follow.

Definition of a devotee: someone who keeps hitting the earth with his golf swing.

Someone once asked a bad golfer what his handicap was. 'Honesty,' he said.

Scientific law of golf. The hole is always greater than the sum of the constituent putts.

The trouble with golf is that by the time a player can afford to lose the ball he can't hit that far!

The golf course consists of 18 holes, 17 of them unnecessary but included simply to multiply frustration.

If the universe if finite, as some people claim, how come golfers never find all those balls they lose?

Mind may be control over matter, but not when it comes to golf.

Would you say that golf is just another way of beating around the bush?

Golf is unlike politics insofar as you can't improve your lie in golf . . .

Old golfers never die, they simply lose their balls.

Golf is like a love affair. If you don't take it seriously it's no fun. If you do it breaks you heart.

Would you say a golfer is a man who putts it around?

Did you hear about the fat golfer? When he put the ball where he could see it he couldn't hit it and when he put it where he could hit it, he couldn't see it!

A cricket commentator on the radio once said, 'And 33 runs have been scored, shared equally between the two batsmen.' He later followed it up with, 'The batsman throws his head back and it goes through to the keeper.'

The local cricket club is like an old bra — no cups and hardly any support.

Did you hear about the Irish rugby match? The players swapped jerseys at half time.

Sign in the toilets of a Scottish rugby club: Please don't put cigarette ends in the urinals. It makes them soggy and difficult to light.

Would you say that rugby is a game played by gentlemen with odd shaped balls?

Have you heard about the new self-help group called Anglers Anonymous? You phone them up and listen to a pack of lies.

To have good fortune when fishing, you have to get there yesterday when the fish were biting.

An optimist may be defined as a person who takes a camera with him when he goes fishing.

Anglers catch their biggest fish by the tale ...

A fisherman has a whole year of fun — ten days fishing and 355 days fiddling with his tackle.

All fish gain weight slowly, except for those that got away.

Fishing is generally better before you get there or after you leave.

How far a fisherman stretches the truth depends on the length of his arms.

Did you hear about the snooker player who set out to improve his game? He started smoking pot.

Another snooker player arrived home after a very successful evening during which he'd managed to sink seven pints and three double whiskies ...

Would you say the SAS smoke more embassies than Hurricane Higgins?

Don't believe that swimming is good for the figure. Have you ever seen a whale?

Did you see the big boxing match on TV last night? The boxer in the black shorts did so much bobbing and weaving that by the end of the fight he'd made a carpet.

In the loos of Wimbledon some bright spark has written on one wall, *For the rules of tennis see wall opposite*. And on the other wall, *For the rules of tennis see wall opposite*.

Snoopy on tennis: It doesn't matter if you win or lose — until you lose.

Nothing keeps an athletics crowd's attention more than a cross-eyed javelin thrower.

Gambling can be a messy business. Did you hear about the pigeon that put all he had on Lester Piggott?

What about the man who started manufacturing boomerangs? He said the sport was making a comeback.

The chap who kept racing pigeons was a bitterly disappointed man. He never caught one.

An Irishman who heard about the latest craze for ice hockey began to make his own sticks. Problem was, they kept melting in his hands . . .

Pity the unfortunate sailor who was thrown out of the singlehanded yacht race for using both hands . . .

Seen in a newspaper: One-armed tennis title changes hands.

Graffiti: Mallet rules, croquet?

The reason a woman can't catch a ball as well as a man is that a man is much bigger and easier to catch.

If at first you don't succeed, so much for sky-diving.

COMIC SPEECHES FOR ALL OCCASIONS

Michael Kilgarriff

TAKE THE TERROR OUT OF SPEECHMAKING

The speeches people always remember are the funny ones — but that does not make them any easier to deliver. So if your progress on the rostrum or at the dinner table, by the wedding cake or at the local is dogged by trembling kneecaps and notes quivering like aspen leaves in a Force 10 gale, you need COMIC SPEECHES FOR ALL OCCASIONS.

Michael Kilgarriff, the actor, comedian, old time music hall chairman, cabaret artist and seasonal pantomime giant gives foolproof advice on all aspects of speechmaking: how to project your voice, how to handle hecklers, how to time your punch lines, which jokes to use and which subjects to avoid.

Futura Publications
Non-Fiction/Humour
0 7088 1460 3

THE BOOK OF HEROIC FAILURES

Stephen Pile

'Are you fed up with all those books telling you how to be successful? Are you dreadful at most things you try? Here at long last is a book in praise of spectacular failure and people who can't do a thing'
Namib Times

'One of the few books to make me laugh out loud'
Sunday Express

'One of the funniest and most entertaining books I have dipped into for a long time'
Country Life

'(A) splendid panorama of non-achievement'
Sunday Telegraph

'As a serious book it's a failure, as a tonic to make your ribs ache, it's a rip-roaring success'
Manchester Evening News

'A disaster'
Stephen Pile

Futura Publications
Non-Fiction
0 7088 1908 7

All Futura Books are available at your bookshop or
newsagent, or can be ordered from the following
address:
Futura Books, Cash Sales Department,
P.O. Box 11, Falmouth, Cornwall TR10 9EN.

Please send cheque or postal order (no currency), and
allow 60p for postage and packing for the first book
plus 25p for the second book and 15p for each additional
book ordered up to a maximum charge of £1.90 in U.K.

B.F.P.O. customers please allow 60p for
the first book, 25p for the second book plus 15p per
copy for the next 7 books, thereafter 9p per book.

Overseas customers including Eire please allow £1.25 for
postage and packing for the first book, 75p for the second
book and 28p for each subsequent title ordered.